FOREST LIFE

PHOTOGRAPHED BY
KIM TAYLOR & JANE BURTON

WRITTEN BY
BARBARA TAYLOR

DK

DORLING KINDERSLEY
LONDON • NEW YORK • STUTTGART

DK

A DORLING KINDERSLEY BOOK

Editor Sue Copsey **Art editor** Val Wright
Senior editor Christiane Gunzi **Designer** Floyd Sayers
Design Assistants Nicola Rawson, Will Wood
Production Louise Barratt
Illustrations Nick Hall
Index Jane Parker
Managing editor Sophie Mitchell
Managing art editor Miranda Kennedy
U.S. editor B. Alison Weir

Consultants
Barry Clarke, Andy Currant, Theresa Greenaway,
Tim Parmenter, Paul Pearce-Kelly, Matthew Robertson, Karen Willson

With thanks to Mike Norton and Surrey Water Gardens for
supplying some of the animals in this book.

Endpapers photographed by Frithjof Skibbe,
Oxford Scientific Films, Ltd.

First American Edition, 1993
10 9 8 7 6 5 4 3 2 1
Published in the United States by
Dorling Kindersley, Inc., 232 Madison Avenue, New York, New York, 10016

Distributed by Houghton Mifflin Company, Boston, Massachusetts.

Library of Congress Cataloging-in-Publication Data
Taylor, Barbara 1954-
Shoreline / Barbara Taylor ; photography by Kim Taylor. – 1st American ed.
p. cm. – (Look closer)
Includes index.
Summary: Discusses the animals and plants that live in forests.
Includes the weasel, giant wood wasp, and the slippery jack mushroom.
ISBN 1-56458-210-8
1. Forest fauna–Juvenile literature. 2. Forest flora–Juvenile literature.
[1. Forest animals. 2. Forest plants.] I. Taylor, Kim, ill. II. Title. III. Series.
QH86.T39 1993
574.909'52–dc20
92-53488-CIP-AC

Color reproduction by Colourscan, Singapore
Printed and bound in Italy by New Interlitho, Milan

CONTENTS

Look for us, and we will show you the size of every animal and plant that you read about in this book.

LIFE IN A FOREST

THE TREES IN A FOREST feed and provide shelter for a huge variety of wildlife, from nesting birds to leaf-eating insects. Some animals live inside the trunk of the tree, while others live among the roots or the leafy branches. Even the rotting logs and leaf litter on the ground are full of tiny animals, and fungi and ferns thrive in the shady, moist environment. Many woodlands have been cut down to make way for factories, farms, and houses. Unless we protect the forests that are left, and plant new trees to replace those that have gone, thousands of plants and animals will lose their homes.

The tawny owl
(Strix aluco)
is 1 ft. high.
It lives in Africa, Asia,
and Europe.

The many-zoned fungus
(Coriolus versicolor)
is 11/4 in. wide.
It lives in Australia and
North of the equator.

The young weasel's
(Mustela nivalis)
body is 6 in. long.
It lives in Asia,
Europe, North Africa,
and North America.

The fly agaric's
(Amanita muscaria)
cap is 2 1/2 in. wide.
It lives in Australia
and West Africa, and
north of the equator.

The brown roll-rim's
(Paxillus involutus)
cap is 2 in. wide.
It lives north of
the equator.

The common centipede
(Lithobius forficatus)
is 1 1/4 in. long.
It lives in Europe.

The eastern rosella
(Platycercus eximius)
is 2 ft. long.
It lives in Australia.

The bluebell's
(Hyacinthoides non-scripta)
flower stalk is 8 in. high.
It lives in Europe.

The scaly male fern's
(Dryopteris affinis)
fronds are 10 in. long.
It lives in Europe and
Southwest Asia.

The giant wood wasp
(Urocerus gigas)
is 1 in. long.
It lives in Asia, Europe,
and northern Africa.

The oak bush cricket
(Meconema thalassinum)
is 1/2 in. long.
It lives in Europe and
western Asia.

The young gray squirrel's
(Sciurus carolinensis)
body is 3 in. long.
It lives in Europe, North
America, and Southern Africa.

The slippery jack's
(Suillus luteus)
cap is 2 in. wide.
It lives all over the world.

**The American spotted
salamander's**
(Ambystoma maculatum)
head and body are 6 in. long.
It lives in North America.

WHAT A HOOT

AN UNMISTAKABLE HOOT in the night lets you know that there is a tawny owl in the woods. During the day, the owl sits quietly among the trees. It is hard to spot because its mottled coloring blends in with the bark and leaves. At night, the owl hunts for voles, mice, rats, and small birds. Its sharp hearing and silent flight make it an excellent hunter. Tawny owls nest in hollow trees, or in the old nests of other birds, such as magpies. The female lays between two and four white eggs, and the chicks, called owlets, hatch after about four weeks. The male brings food for the owlets, but sometimes, if prey is hard to find, the biggest owlet eats the smaller ones. The young birds leave the nest after five weeks, but their parents keep feeding them until they are three months old.

GUESS WHAT?
If a flock of small birds spots a tawny owl, they fly around it making a lot of noise. They do this to make the owl move away from their territory (the area where they live). When small birds annoy an enemy in this way, it is called mobbing.

KEEPING QUIET
Tawny owls can fly very quietly. This enables them to hear the squeaks of their prey, and to pounce without warning. There are fluffy, comblike fringes on the feathers that deaden the sound of the wingbeats. Also, the surfaces of the feathers are velvety. This muffles the sound of the feathers brushing against each other, and the air rushing between them.

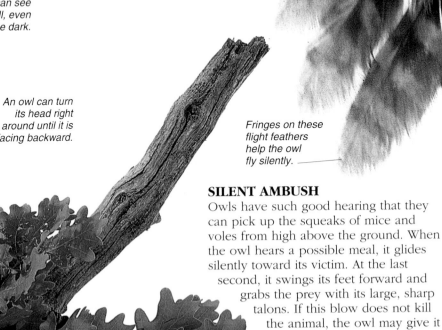

The two large ear openings are hidden behind the feathers on these rounded areas of the face.

These huge eyes face forward. They can see very well, even in the dark.

These downy feathers show that this is a young owl.

An owl can turn its head right around until it is facing backward.

Fringes on these flight feathers help the owl fly silently.

SILENT AMBUSH
Owls have such good hearing that they can pick up the squeaks of mice and voles from high above the ground. When the owl hears a possible meal, it glides silently toward its victim. At the last second, it swings its feet forward and grabs the prey with its large, sharp talons. If this blow does not kill the animal, the owl may give it a sharp bite at the base of the skull.

COUGH MIXTURE
Owls usually swallow their smaller prey whole, gulping down bones, fur, and feathers, as well as flesh. But they cannot digest these parts of their victims, so they cough them up again in the form of large pellets. By looking at the contents of an owl pellet, you can tell what the bird has eaten.

Large, strong wings make this owl a powerful flier.

There is a thick covering of soft feathers on the front of the body to keep the owl warm.

The large feet end in needle-sharp, curved talons for grasping and killing prey.

Feathers down to the toes help protect the owl from the bites of its prey.

THE CRICKET SEASON

DURING THE long summer days, oak bush crickets hide away among the leafy woodland bushes. They come out at night to feed on plants and small insects, or to search for a mate. The male attracts a female by making drumming or scraping sounds. After mating, the female lays her eggs in the soil, inside plant stems, or beneath the bark of a tree. She uses her sharp egg-laying tube, called an ovipositor, to carve a separate space for each egg. The young crickets, called nymphs, hatch the following spring. They look like miniature adults, but they have no wings. Their skin is hard and will not stretch, so in order to grow, they shed their skin several times to reveal a new one underneath. This process is called molting. By late summer, each nymph has molted up to five times. After the final molt it has become a fully grown adult with wings.

FANTASTIC FEELERS

Oak bush crickets are sometimes called long-horned grasshoppers, because of their long, threadlike antennae (feelers). These help the cricket feel its way around in the dark. If the antennae sense an enemy ahead, their length gives the cricket a few extra inches to make its escape.

The large compound eyes can detect movement in almost every direction at the same time.

The bush cricket's ears are on its front legs, just below the knee joints.

A sharp claw on the end of each leg helps the insect grip on to plants.

GUESS WHAT?

The bush cricket's ears are not on its head, but on its front legs instead. The ears are like drum skins, stretched tight across a hollow in the leg. They vibrate when sounds hit them.

LEAFY LOOK-ALIKE

The oak bush cricket blends in well with its leafy green surroundings. Its body is a similar color to the bushes where it lives, and its wings look like leaves. It is difficult for enemies, such as birds, to tell which is a leaf and which is a cricket.

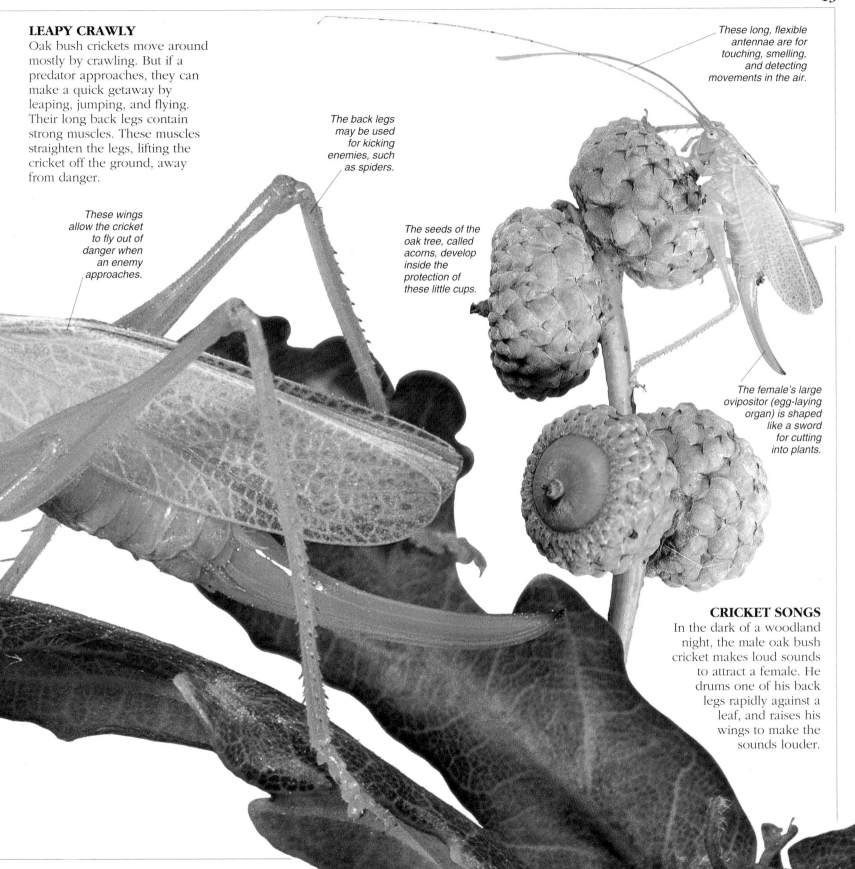

LEAPY CRAWLY

Oak bush crickets move around mostly by crawling. But if a predator approaches, they can make a quick getaway by leaping, jumping, and flying. Their long back legs contain strong muscles. These muscles straighten the legs, lifting the cricket off the ground, away from danger.

These long, flexible antennae are for touching, smelling, and detecting movements in the air.

The back legs may be used for kicking enemies, such as spiders.

These wings allow the cricket to fly out of danger when an enemy approaches.

The seeds of the oak tree, called acorns, develop inside the protection of these little cups.

The female's large ovipositor (egg-laying organ) is shaped like a sword for cutting into plants.

CRICKET SONGS

In the dark of a woodland night, the male oak bush cricket makes loud sounds to attract a female. He drums one of his back legs rapidly against a leaf, and raises his wings to make the sounds louder.

STOP AND START

THE GRAY SQUIRREL travels nimbly through the trees in search of food. If danger threatens, it may stay completely still, relying on its mottled gray color to hide it against tree trunks. But if it is spotted by an enemy, such as a bird of prey, the squirrel's speedy acrobatics make it difficult to catch. The gray squirrel builds a round, football-sized nest, called a drey, in the fork of a tree. The drey is made of twigs, and lined with soft materials, such as grass and leaves. In spring, and often in summer, too, the female gives birth to two or three young. At first, they have no fur and cannot see. After two or three months, the young squirrels leave the drey and begin to fend for themselves.

The top layer of fur is made up of long, stiff hairs. Close up, you can see that these outer hairs are colored brown, black, and white.

Long, strong claws grip tightly onto smooth, slippery branches.

Squirrels sit up to feed, holding food in their front paws.

If the squirrel spots an enemy, it may warn others by displaying this patch of white fur.

These long back feet help the animal balance.

NUT NIBBLER
Trees provide squirrels with food all year-round. In fall and winter, they feed mainly on fruit and seeds, such as acorns, beechnuts, and pinecones. In spring and summer, squirrels eat catkins and buds, and strip the bark from trees in order to feed on the juicy sap underneath. Gray squirrels also eat fungi, insects, and young birds.

SQUIRREL SIGNALS
Gray squirrels use sounds, scents, and body language, such as flapping the tail, to communicate with each other. These signals tell other squirrels about food, warn them of danger, or attract a mate.

GUESS WHAT?

Gray squirrels can run at speeds of up to 18 mph. They are also good swimmers. They use their back feet to paddle themselves along, and hold their tail above the water like a bushy sail.

TIGHTROPE TRICKS

Squirrels leap gracefully from branch to branch, using their tails like rudders to change direction. They can balance on the flimsiest of twigs, and easily run up and down smooth tree trunks by clinging on with their sharp claws. On the ground, squirrels often stop and sit upright to sniff the air for danger.

SURVIVAL SKILLS

In winter, the gray squirrel spends much of its time sheltering in its drey. Before the cold weather arrives, the squirrel eats as much food as it can to build up stores of fat in its body. This will help it survive when food is hard to find. It also buries nuts in the ground, and uses its excellent sense of smell to find them again.

Grayish-brown fur helps hide the squirrel among bark and leaves.

Long, sensitive whiskers help the squirrel feel its way around.

These young squirrels are just a few months old.

Squirrels can fluff up their tails to make themselves look larger and more fearsome.

A NIGHT OUT

ON COOL, WET NIGHTS, the spotted salamander
comes out of its forest burrow to hunt for a meal. It makes no
sound, unlike its noisy relatives, the frogs and toads. In spring,
spotted salamanders travel to a nearby pond, often in large groups,
to mate and lay their eggs. Each female lays about 100 eggs in a
jelly-covered mass. One or two months later, the young, called
larvae, hatch out into the water. They have a head and a long tail,
and breathe through gills, like fish. They are carnivorous (meat-
eating), and feed on small water insects. Over the next few
months they develop legs, and their gills are replaced by lungs
inside their bodies for breathing air. Eventually, the young
salamanders climb out of the pond to begin life on land.

DANGER SPOTS
The two rows of bright
yellow spots on this
salamander's body warn
enemies, such as birds and
snakes, to leave it alone. If it is
attacked, a milky poison oozes out
of special glands at the back of its
head. The poison tastes nasty, so
the enemy usually looks
somewhere else for a meal.

*Fungi such as
this mushroom
also live in damp,
shady places.*

*Yellow spots
warn enemies
that this
salamander
is poisonous.*

*The eyes can
see well in
the dark.*

DOWN UNDER
Spotted salamanders
live on land, but they
have to stay in damp
places. This is because their
skin is not waterproof, and it
cannot keep in moisture. If a
salamander's skin dries out, it
will die. For this reason it spends
most of its time buried beneath
the soil, or under a log or a rock.

*The streamlined shape of
the salamander's s body
and tail help it burrow
under logs and
rocks, and
through soil.*

*The feet end in
long, splayed toes
for shoveling the
soil aside.*

The salamander's smooth, moist skin helps it slither through soil easily.

GUESS WHAT?
Spotted salamanders have become rare in many areas. This is because the ponds in which they lay their eggs have been polluted by acid rain, which can kill the young.

SLIPPERY SKIN
The salamander's skin is delicate, and sometimes gets damaged as the animal burrows beneath the ground. So every week or two, the outer layer of skin is shed to reveal a new one that has grown underneath. This is called molting.

Adult salamanders have lungs, but they can also breathe through their thin skin.

AFTERNOON SNACK
The spotted salamander usually waits for nightfall before it comes out of its damp hiding place. But sometimes, on rainy days, it lurks in the mouth of its burrow. There it waits to pounce on unsuspecting prey. Small creatures such as insects, worms, slugs, and snails are quickly snapped up in its hungry jaws.

FABULOUS FUNGI

LIKE LITTLE UMBRELLAS, toadstools sprout from
tree trunks, branches, and leaf litter on the woodland
floor. Mushrooms and toadstools belong to a group
of organisms called fungi. Fungi feed on plants and
animals, both living and dead, whereas most plants
make their food from air, water, and minerals. The main
part of the fungus is hidden away inside whatever it is
living on, such as a tree. It is made of a network of fine,
branching threads, called hyphae. These are grouped together
in a cobweblike net, called a mycelium. When a fungus is
ready to reproduce, it forms fruit bodies, such as toadstools,
above the surface. These can be all sorts of shapes, depending
on the kind of fungus. Each fruit body contains millions of
tiny spores, which are blown away by the wind, or carried off
by animals that like to feed on the fungus. If the spores land
in a suitable spot, they grow into new fungi.

*These frills are
found on many
kinds of fungi.
They are called
gills, because they
look like the gills
of a fish.*

RECYCLING EXPERTS

Without fungi, the woodland
would soon be buried under piles
of dead leaves and other plant and
animal remains. As the fungi feed
on this dead and decaying material,
they release some of the nutrients
back into the soil. Plants take
up these nutrients through
their roots as they grow.
So the fungi recycle
materials that can be used
over and over again.

*This fungus is called
slippery jack. Its name
comes from the
slimy covering on
its cap. It grows
beneath conifers,
such as Scotch
pine trees.*

*This ring shows where
the cap used to be
joined to the stalk
while the fruit body
was developing.*

*The spores are
produced in masses
of fine tubes
under the cap.*

At first, the fly agaric fungus is round, white, and egg-like. Then it grows a stalk with a rounded cap. Finally it develops into a flat-capped toadstool with a dip in the middle.

GUESS WHAT?
Poisonous fungi are often called toadstools. Some kinds of toadstools are so deadly that once they have been eaten, there is no cure. Never touch a wild mushroom or toadstool without checking with an expert that it is not poisonous.

FLY KILLER

The bright red, poisonous fly agaric often lives on the roots of birch trees. The tree makes sugars that it stores in its roots, and the fungus takes some of these sugars to feed on. In return, the fly agaric helps the tree take up minerals from the soil, so both the tree and the fungus benefit from living together. Fly agaric gets its name from its use as a fly killer. People used to mix it with milk and sugar to make a sweet but deadly liquid, which flies loved to drink.

TRUNK TROUBLE

Some fungi produce fruit bodies that are shaped like shelf brackets. This is why they are called bracket fungi. These fungi often grow out of living tree trunks. In most cases, they eventually kill the tree. Other kinds of bracket fungi, like this many-zoned fungus, grow on dead tree stumps and fallen logs.

These white spots are the remains of the skin that covered the growing toadstool. They may be washed off by heavy rain.

This poisonous brown roll-rim is a good example of a funnel-shaped toadstool.

This kind of bracket fungus is called many-zoned, because it has different bands of color.

Frilly gills run down the stem of the brown roll-rim fungus. The spores fall from the edges of the gills.

Many-zoned fungus grows throughout the year on all kinds of dead wood.

DRILLER WASPS

ON SUNNY SUMMER days, male giant wood wasps fly around the treetops looking for a mate. Meanwhile, the females search for conifer trees to lay their eggs in. After mating, each female drills narrow tunnels deep inside a tree using her long ovipositor. Then she lays one egg inside each hole. The females usually choose dead or dying trees, because the wood is softer for boring holes in. Two or three days later, caterpillarlike larvae (grubs) hatch, and begin to chew away at the wood. Each larva grows very slowly because wood is hard to digest, and is not very nutritious. About two years later the larva starts to burrow its way out of the tree, stopping just below the surface. Then it spins a cocoon made of silk and bits of chewed wood. After several months, the cocoon splits and the adult wasp climbs out. It gnaws a short tunnel to escape, then flies off to find a mate.

GUESS WHAT?
Sometimes trees are chopped down with developing wood wasp larvae inside them. These trees may be cut up into planks for building houses or making furniture. A year or two later, an adult giant wood wasp may suddenly climb out.

STRIPY TRICKS
Wasps and bees that can sting often have bright yellow and black stripes. These colors warn enemies that they are dangerous, and should be left alone. Giant wood wasps cannot sting, but they have similar striped coloring. This may fool enemies into thinking that they are dangerous.

The long, thin antennae are for feeling and smelling.

The compound eyes are made up of lots of lenses that build a complete picture, like a jigsaw.

Sensitive hairs pick up information about the surroundings.

Two pairs of delicate, transparent (clear) wings are supported by stiff veins.

The thin legs are made up of several segments. They can bend at the joints.

HARMLESS HORNTAIL
Giant wood wasps are sometimes called horntails, because of the sharp spike at the end of the female's abdomen (rear part of the body). Below this spike is the long egg-laying tube, called the ovipositor. This ovipositor looks much like a fearsome stinger, but in fact it is quite harmless.

FRIENDLY FUNGUS

The female wood wasp eats a fungus that she stores in her body. When she lays her eggs, she coats them with spores. These grow into fungus in the tunnels that the wasp larvae live in. In this way, the wood wasp and fungus help each other. The wasp carries the fungus to its woody home, and the fungus breaks down the wood into a substance that the larvae can eat.

This long, strong ovipositor is for drilling holes and laying eggs.

WAKEFUL WEASEL

BY DAY AND BY NIGHT, these agile weasels run and bound through the forest. They climb well, using their sharp claws to grip smooth or slippery surfaces. Although a weasel is very small, it is a ferocious hunter of other small animals. It is very strong for its size and a male can even kill animals larger than itself, such as young rabbits, when smaller prey is hard to find. In spring, and sometimes in late summer, too, female weasels give birth to a litter of between four and six young, called kittens, in an underground den. The young weasels grow fast and are soon able to join in hunting trips. When they are only three to four months old, they can fend for themselves.

SMALL AND SLENDER
The weasel's long, slender body and short legs help it crawl down small holes, and into cracks in rocks. Females and young weasels, such as this one, can easily follow a mouse or a vole into its burrow and kill it there.

Weasels are very alert and inquisitive. They often stand up on their hind legs to have a good look around.

A weasel's sense of smell is very good.

The weasel's thick, muscular neck allows it to keep a tight hold on a mouse or vole.

A small, slim body like this loses heat quickly. So weasels must eat often in order to keep warm.

These sharp claws grip surfaces and hold on to prey.

GUESS WHAT?
After a meal, a weasel often sleeps in the burrow of its prey. It may even make its home there, lining the burrow with the animal's fur to help keep in warmth.

WINTER WHITE
In cold climates, where it often snows, the weasel molts (sheds) its brown fur, and grows a white coat for the winter months. This makes it hard for prey and predators to see it against the snowy background. In spring, the weasel grows brown fur on its back once more.

FIERCE HUNTER
Weasels usually hunt alone. But when there are young, the family hunts together, so that the young get some practice before they go off on their own. Adult males catch rats, moles, and toads, as well as insects. Weasels kill small prey by biting it on the back of the neck. But if the prey is large, a weasel attacks the less protected throat.

The ears listen for rustling noises made by prey in the undergrowth.

The weasel's fur coat keeps its body warm and protects its skin from scratches.

The weasel's sensitive whiskers help it find its way around, especially in the dark.

SUPER SWOOPER

EASTERN ROSELLAS swoop through open woodlands, making bright splashes of color against the trees. They call to other rosellas to let them know when they have found something to eat, and they screech to warn of danger. Eastern rosellas live in pairs or in small groups. In spring, the male puts on a dramatic performance to attract a mate. He droops his wings, fluffs up his breast feathers, and moves his fanned-out tail from side to side. After a male and female have mated, they usually stay together for the rest of their lives. They find a hole in a eucalyptus tree, where the female lays between four and seven white eggs. The male brings food for the female while she sits on the eggs to keep them warm. After the eggs have hatched, the parents look after their young until they are old enough to fly off on their own.

Sharp, beady eyes spot food easily.

The two outer toes point backward and the two inner toes point forward. This gives a strong hold on twigs and branches.

The rosella's beak never stops growing. If it did, the bird would soon wear it out, cracking seeds.

These sharp claws hold on tightly.

The flight feathers are strong and flexible, so they will not snap when the rosella flaps its wings.

The feathers overlap, so the body is a streamlined shape for flying fast.

HOOKING UP
Rosellas' toes curl around branches with a powerful, vice-like grip. Their long claws also help them get a firm hold, especially on smooth or slippery surfaces. When a rosella climbs up a tree, it hooks its beak around branches to pull itself upward.

HELPFUL HINGES
The rosella's short, thick beak is not firmly attached to its skull. Instead, both parts are hinged, so that they can move separately from the head. This makes it easier for the rosella to grasp and hold food.

The rosella spreads out its tail for support as it climbs.

FRUIT AND NUT

This rosella feeds mainly on seeds. It uses its strong beak like a nutcracker to break them open. Then it pulls out the kernel with its thick, knobby tongue. The rosella also eats fruit, nectar, and insects. To eat a piece of fruit, it makes a hole in the skin with its sharp beak. Then it scoops out the soft flesh inside the fruit.

There are nostrils on top of the beak for smelling food.

The beak is made of keratin, just like your fingernails.

Male rosellas like this one show off their brightly colored feathers to attract a mate.

GUESS WHAT?

The eastern rosella is a kind of parrot. So many parrots have been taken from the wild for people to keep as pets, that several kinds are in danger of becoming extinct. They are also threatened by the destruction of their woodland homes.

EARLY RISERS

IN THE FIRST FEW WEEKS of spring, the forest floor is carpeted with early flowers, such as bluebells and primroses. The leaves fall off the trees in autumn, and provide food for many tiny creatures, such as beetles and other insect larvae. Then flowering plants use the early spring sunshine to bloom and produce seeds before the trees grow new leaves and cover the woodland floor in shade. Bluebells grow from seeds at first, then usually regrow their leaves and flowers each year from the bulbs that form in the soil. Ferns produce simple spores, which do not have their own food supply as seeds do. The plant flicks the spores out, and the wind spreads them. Each spore grows into a tiny, leaflike plant and a new fern grows from this.

The female part, called the stigma, receives pollen from other flowers.

The buds stand up at first, but when the flowers open, they hang downward.

The color around the veins gives this green-veined white butterfly its name.

Each plant has a single flower stalk, with up to 20 flowers. All the flowers grow on one side of the stalk.

On warm days there are plenty of insects around, such as this butterfly, to carry pollen from flower to flower.

Bluebell leaves grow straight up from the bulb.

The narrow leaves push up through the leaf litter in spring.

Bluebells are also called wild hyacinths. The flowers are usually violet-blue, like these, but they can be white or pink also.

SEED BOXES

Bluebells form seeds inside capsules, which are like little boxes with three compartments. When the seeds are ripe they are shiny and black. Then the box splits open so that the seeds can fall to the ground and grow into new plants.

CURLY CROZIERS

Fern leaves grow from a swollen underground stem called a rhizome, which contains stored food. In spring, the young leaves slowly unfurl. They look like little hooks, and they are called croziers, after the crook that a bishop carries during ceremonies. The curled shape helps prevent the soft young leaflets from drying out.

This fern is just beginning to unfurl. The fronds sometimes grow for up to two years before they appear above the ground.

The six petals curl back at the tip, forming a bell shape, so the pollen sacs on the stamens stick out of the flower.

UNDERGROUND PANTRY

Bluebells survive winter as small, white, egg-shaped bulbs buried in the soil. These bulbs contain food that the plant makes and stores during the summer. In spring, the first new leaves use the energy in the stored food to grow.

GUESS WHAT?

Prehistoric ferns grew as big as trees, and formed the world's first forests. Their remains are part of the coal that we burn as fuel today.

Sometimes buds grow out of the rhizome and develop into new plants. What looks like a large fern is often several plants growing together.

DANGER IN THE DARK

DURING THE DAY, COMMON centipedes hide away in dark, damp places on the forest floor. They lie under fallen leaves, logs, or stones, where they are safe from enemies, such as birds. Centipedes come out at night to hunt. They eat insects, worms, spiders, slugs, and even other centipedes. In spring or summer, female centipedes lay their eggs, then cover them with soil to keep them hidden from enemies. When the young hatch out, they have only seven body segments and seven pairs of legs. Their outer skin, called the exoskeleton, is hard and cannot stretch. So every now and again, as a centipede grows bigger, it molts (sheds its skin). After each of the first four molts, the centipede has more body segments, all with a pair of legs. When this common centipede has molted four times, it has 15 segments and a full set of 30 legs.

There is a pair of legs on every segment of the body. Except for the pair on the last segment, they are all walking legs.

The centipede can squeeze its flat body under stones, bark, and leaves, and through soil.

The legs are made up of several sections, and all of the joints can bend.

The claw at the end of each leg helps the centipede grip wood and stones.

The last two legs have sharp tips, which put off enemies attacking from behind.

LANKY LEGS
The centipede's many legs allow it to move quickly over the forest floor. The legs are long, so they can take large strides. As the centipede runs along, each leg overlaps the one in front. But the legs are longer toward the back, so each foot steps out more to the side than the one in front of it. This means that the animal does not trip over its own legs.

COOL CUSTOMER

Centipedes do not have a waterproof layer on their bodies as insects and spiders do. They can easily dry out, so they live in damp places where they do not lose too much moisture. Centipedes stay out of direct sunlight, and only hunt at night when the air is cool and moist.

Long antennae (feelers) help the centipede feel its way around in the dark.

Tiny hairs on the centipede's legs give it extra grip for running fast.

MOONLIGHT MURDER

This animal is a fierce hunter. It has a pair of large, curved claws underneath the head, which it uses to grab prey. Centipedes paralyze their victims by injecting them with poison from fangs at the end of the claws. When the victim has stopped moving, the centipede tears it apart with its strong mouthparts.

A tough outer layer, called the exoskeleton, protects the centipede's soft body.

Close up, you can just see tiny hairs on the antennae. These hairs are very sensitive to touch.

Each antenna is divided into many segments, so it can bend easily.

GUESS WHAT?

The name centipede means "a hundred feet." But the number of feet varies from one kind of centipede to another. Some may have more than 300 feet, but others, such as this common centipede, have only 30.

GLOSSARY

Abdomen *the rear part of the body*
Antennae *a pair of feelers*
Bulb *the underground part of some plants, which contains stored food energy*
Compound eyes *eyes that consist of many separate lenses*
Drey *a squirrel's nest*
Exoskeleton *a tough covering on the body, made of a substance called chitin*
Gills *the organs that animals, such as fish, use to take in oxygen from the water*
Hyphae *the thin, underground threads of a fungus*
Keratin *the substance that makes up hair, fur, and nails*
Larva *the young, grublike stage of an animal, such as an insect*
Mandibles *a pair of mouthparts for biting and chewing*

Molt *to shed the skin or exoskeleton*
Mycelium *the mass of hyphae that makes up the body of a fungus*
Nymph *the larva of certain kinds of insects, such as crickets*
Ovipositor *the egg-laying tube at the tip of the abdomen in most female insects*
Rhizome *a thick underground stem in some plants, where food is stored*
Spores *seedlike bodies produced by many plants and simple animals when the male and female sex cells pair*
Stamen *the male part of a flower, where pollen is produced*
Stigma *the female part of a flower, which collects the pollen*
Talon *the sharp, hooked claw of a bird*
Streamlined *a shape that moves easily through air, water, or soil*